Poems Across the Pavement

Poems
across the
pavement

25TH ANNIVERSARY EDITION

LUIS J
RODRIGUEZ

TIA CHUCHA PRESS

Printed in the United States of America

ISBN 978-1-882688-48-7

Book designer: Jane Brunette
Front cover photo: Violet Soto
Back cover photo of Luis J. Rodriguez: Gerardo Serna

ISBN 0-9624287-0-1 / ISBN-13 978-0-9624287-0-8
Library of Congress Catalog Card Number 90-119897

Cover art for first through fourth editions: Gamaliel Ramirez

Published by:
Tia Chucha Press
A Project of Tia Chucha's Centro Cultural & Bookstore
PO Box 328
San Fernando CA 91341

Distributed by:
Northwestern University Press
Chicago Distribution Center
11030 S. Langley
Chicago IL 60628

Grants from the City of Chicago, Department of Cultural Affairs, Office of Fine Arts; the Illinois Arts Council; and the National Endowment for the Arts supported the original publication of this book. Tia Chucha's Centro Cultural & Bookstore is a 501 (c) (3) tax-exempt organization supported by the California Community Foundation, California Arts Council, Los Angeles County Arts Commission, Los Angeles City Department of Cultural Affairs, the Annenberg Foundation, the Lia Fund, the Attias Family Foundation, the Guacamole Fund, and the Weingart Foundation, among others. And donations from Bruce Springsteen, John Densmore of The Doors, Jackson Brown, Lou Adler, Richard Foos, Gary Stewart, Luis and Trini Rodriguez, and more.

Contents

For my children:
Ramiro Daniel
Andrea Victoria
Ruben Joaquin
&
Luis Jacinto

What the River Says, That is What I Say

Introduction to the 25th Anniversary Edition

I will listen to what you say.
You and I can run and look
at the silent river and wait. We know
the current is there, hidden; and there
are comings and goings from miles away
that hold the stillness exactly before us.
What the river says, that is what I say.
—WILLIAM STAFFORD

W HEN I first published *Poems across the Pavement*, I was a 35-year-old unknown writer hungry for the power of words, metaphors and images, for the purposeful agreements that keep people in life, in art, in the realms of meaning and connection. For years I labored in a primary passion—the often turbulent but also stilled waters of poetry and story—to lift the oppressive weight of diminishment and anonymity.

You could say I was nobody, nowhere, nothing. Yet through language this became a liberating experience. Unseen and unheard are often the most powerful sources of the most compelling writing.

I'm talking about mouthless souls that have found vision and voice as far back as the first

9

African griots to the Hip Hop artists, performance poets, and multi-genre writers of today.

I have been writing since my teens, scribbles really, of ideas, thoughts, imaginings. I was a troubled barrio gang member and drug addict. Some of these scribblings emerged in juvenile hall, in a county jail cellblock, or in the dank streets of downtown Los Angeles as I wandered homeless. A few verses sprouted while I lay in a sparse room of my family's garage with no heat and only a piss bucket and a bunk.

When I was 18, vignettes called "Barrio Expressions" were published in a Chicano literary magazine from Berkeley CA called *Quinto Sol*. Over the years, sporadic pieces found their way into magazines, newspapers and books when I lived in Los Angeles, the Bay Area, the Inland Empire, and Chicago. Finally I self-published *Poems across the Pavement*, also serving as the first book of a 25-year publishing venture—Tia Chucha Press—that to date has produced more than 50 poetry collections, anthologies, chapbooks, and a CD.

A personal quest aligned with social necessity.

By 2001 this journey lead to the creation of Tia Chucha's Café Cultural in the San Fernando Valley section of Los Angeles, which later became the nonprofit Tia Chucha's Centro Cultural & Bookstore—in twelve years we've raised more than a million dollars for community-based arts, music, theater, writing, indigenous cosmology & dance, and healing workshops as well as festivals, Open Mics, author readings, mural projects, youth empowerment work, films, and books & more books.

My own output now consist of fifteen books in poetry, fiction, children's literature, and nonfiction—and countless pieces in anthologies, textbooks, readers, and more.

For twenty years, I've made a living—and contributed to social and artistic change—as a writer, editor, lecturer, and organizer. I've been my own boss. And in the process I've gained a personal authority that is part and parcel of the authority inherent in any community or social class trying to break out of its bonds, trying to carve a path out of no path. Many poets and artists in our culture are often floating in the world, desperate for ground, an audience, a lasting attachment. Most end up exiled to the outskirts, the streets, hidden in bars, libraries or cafes, or alone in the many rooms of an internal house, seemingly without story or song or the stillness before an epiphany.

I had to break out somehow or I was going to fade away in drugs, in drink, in the intoxication of impulsive love, in the eyes of despair. Poetry saved my life. And this book in your hand, these 19 poems, finding heart and home, became the birth of a presumably impossible blossom.

As long as I can hear the river, I'll have much to say.

—*Luis J. Rodriguez*
November 2013

Running to America

For Alfonso
and Maria Estela Rodriguez,
migrants

They are night shadows violating borders,
fingers curled through chain-link fences,
hiding from infra-red eyes, dodging 30-30 bullets.
They leave familiar smells, warmth and sounds
as ancient as the trampled stones.

Running to America.

There is a woman in her finest border-crossing wear:
A purple blouse from an older sister,
a pair of worn shoes from a church bazaar,
a tattered coat from a former lover.

There is a child dressed in black,
fear sparkling from dark Indian eyes,
clinging to a headless Barbie doll.

And the men, some hardened, quiet,
others young and loud—you see something
like this in prisons. Soon they will cross
on their bellies, kissing black earth,

then run to America.

Strange voices whisper behind garbage cans,
beneath freeway passes, next to broken bottles.
The spatter of words, textured and multi-colored,
invoke demons.

They must run to America.

Their skin, color of earth, is a brand
for all the great ranchers, for the killing floors
on Soto Street and as slaughter
for the garment row. Still they come:
A hungry people have no country.

Their tears are the grease of the bobbing machines
that rip into cloth
that make clothes
that keep you warm.

They have endured the sun's stranglehold,
el cortito, foundry heats and dark caves
of mines, swallowing men.

Still they come, wandering bravely
through the thickness of this strange land's
maddening ambivalence.

Their cries are singed with fires of hope.
Their babies are born with a lion
in their hearts.

Who can confine them?
Who can tell them
which lines never to cross?

For the green rivers, for their looted gold,
escaping the blood of a land
that threatens to drown them,
they have come,

running to America.

I Hear a Saxophone

SWEET MUSIC CAME IN
THROUGH THE SIDE WINDOW
OF A THREE-STORY FLAT.
THE POEM CAME NEXT.

I hear a saxophone
crying out tunes
in deep colors,
of blues
of reds
of yellows.

Every street voice,
every longing child,
every mother's song,
blends through
this brass throat,

stirring dust
coalescing with
a cat's perverted wail,
tires screeching,
a Spanish curse
floating through thin walls.

I hear a saxophone,
plucking notes
from heart beats,
a cacophony of crippled cries.

Echoes, echoes, echoes…
pounding into a purified exchange
between woodwind
and soul.

String Bean

THANKS TO
REYNALDA PALACIOS

1.

Come to this shrine, a living room altar,
a raised place for statues of santos
surrounded by candles,
adorned with rosary beads and flowers.

Come. Touch the icons
of *La Virgen de Guadalupe*,
Niño Jesus and a doll-like figure of *San Judas*,
each with outstretched hands
and small flowing robes.

Come hear *mi ama's* encantations,
lighting candles over expressionless face,
over painted blood
on a bust of a blue-eyed Jesus.

Mi ama—always on her knees,
either praying or scrubbing floors.

2.
Next to *La Virgen*, in a place of near sainthood,
stood a portrait of my Indian grandmother.
Mama prayed to her.

She prayed for food
on the days in-between my father's lay-offs.
She prayed for my brother and me,
who played in the hidden spaces
of sewer tunnel and hobo nest
by the railroad tracks.
She prayed we would come home
without blood pouring from a wound.

She prayed for her daughters,
a common prayer for all women.
She prayed they'd grow up unviolated
in spirit, body or mind.
She prayed for the kind of strength
that had taken Mama through a drunken father,
nightly beatings, and seeing her mother
dragged around the house by the hair.

3.
Sundays in the *barrio*
people emerged from lop-sided and peeling
wood-frame homes in the finest attire.
They converged on the church.
Even the craziest dudes had *La Virgen*
tattooed on their backs.
Every time somebody cruised by the church
they crossed themselves.

4.
Children piled into Sunday school classes.
Nuns in black with wrinkled faces
punished kids for speaking out,
for laughing behind their backs or being late.

There are bottle caps where children knelt,
missals held in outstretched hands,
for what seemed hours.

One time a nun asked a little girl,
"Who is God?"
The girl rose from her seat,
nervous, fearful.
Finally, after a slow start, she replied,
"God ees a string bean."
The class exploded into an uproar.
The nun gasped in horror.

She grabbed a ruler from her desk,
rushed up to the trembling girl
and swung it down onto the inside of the girl's hand.
It took a while before the nun realized
the girl had meant to say,
"God is a supreme being."

Rosalie has Candles

Rosalie has candles in a circle around her bed.
One night as I lay on a couch in a tequila stupor,
she takes off my shoes and trousers,
pulls a cover over me and snips two inches of hair
from my head. She places the hair in a glass
near the candles. I don't know why.
I don't know why she searches for me.
I don't know how she finds me in the bars.
I don't know why she ridicules the women I like
and uses me to meet men.
Rosalie usually finds solace in a glass
of whiskey. In my face she finds the same thing.
I don't know why. We argue too much.
We feign caring and then hurt each other
with indifference. With others we are tough
and mean. But in the quiet of darkness
we hold each other and caress like kittens.
She says she can only make love to someone
when she is drunk. She says she loves men
but has lesbian friends.
She loves being looked at. I want to hide.
She hates struggle. That's all I do.
She has Gods to pray to. I just curse.
I don't know what she sees in my face,
or hands for that matter. I only know
she needs me like whiskey.

The Monster

It erupted into our lives:
Two guys in jeans shoved it through the door
—heaving & grunting & biting lower lips.

A large industrial sewing machine.
We called it "the monster."

It came on a winter's day,
rented out of mother's pay.
Once in the living room
the walls seemed to cave in around it.

Black footsteps to our door
brought heaps of cloth for Mama to sew.
Noises of war burst out of the living room.
Rafters rattled. Floors farted
—the radio going into static
each time the needle ripped into fabric.

Many nights I'd get up from bed,
wander squinty-eyed down a hallway
and peer through a dust-covered blanket
to where Mama and the monster
did nightly battle.

I could see Mama through the yellow haze
of a single light bulb.
She slouched over the machine.
Her eyes almost closed.
Her hair in disheveled braids,

each stitch binding her life
to scraps of cloth.

"Race" Politics

FOR MY BROTHER,
"THE FROG"

My brother and I
—shopping for *la jefita*—
decided to get the "good food"
over on the other side of the tracks.

We dared each other, laughed a little.
Thought about this. Said, what's the big deal?
Thought about that. Decided we were men,
not boys. Decided we should go wherever
we damn wanted to.

Oh, my brother—now he was bad.
Tough dude. Afraid of nothing.
I was afraid of him.

So there we go, climbing over
the iron and wood ties, over discarded sofas
and bent-up market carts,
over a weed-and-dirt road,
into a place called South Gate
—all white, all American.

We entered the forbidden narrow line of hate,
imposed, transposed, supposed,
a line of power/powerlessness
full of meaning, meaning nothing

—those lines that crisscross the abdomen
of this land, that strangle you in your days,
in your nights. When you dream.

There we were, two Mexicans,
six and nine—from Watts no less.
Oh, this was plenty reason to hate us.

Plenty reason to run up behind us,
five teenagers on bikes.
Plenty reason to knock the groceries
out of our arms—a splattering heap of soup cans,
bread and candy.

Plenty reason to hold me down on the hot asphalt,
melted gum and chips of broken beer bottle
on my lips and cheek.

Plenty reason to get my brother by the throat,
taking turns punching him in the face, stomach,
cutting his lower lip, punching, him vomiting,
until swollen and dark blue he slid from their grasp
like a rotten banana from its peeling.

When the teens had enough, they threw us back,
dirty and lacerated, back to Watts,
its towers shiny with ceramic and glass embedded
in cement across the orange-red sky.

My brother then forced me to promise
not to tell anyone how he cried.
He forced me to swear to God,
to Jesus Christ, to our long-dead Indian grandmother
—keepers of our meddling souls.

Tombstone Poets

Leaning against fractured tombstones,
we wove poems, Micaela and me,
grabbing strands from sunken lives,
creating an alchemy of words,
interlaced with a needle-induced glow,
sparking prose out of the poverty
of unreason.

Ragged memories pushed tongues
into cheap chatter, recalling port wine,
jail nights—the terror time between
2 am and the first light of day
without lovers.

And the *tecata* look in her smile,
so distant even as she gazed into my eyes,
here beneath an eastside sun.

Precious, precious, precious…
the noon hours at Evergreen cemetery.
Paper lunch bags at our side.

Even now I hear the humming from her soul.

But heroin took her home from me.
Strings of words suspended in mist
like broken webs.
Only protruding headstones remain,

mute witnesses to when life glowed afire,
when Micaela and I wove tempestuous silk
leaning on slabs of chipped stone.

Lucinda

Santa Ana winds forced my VW bug
to dance across Interstate 10
as I drove for hours toward home.

To your door,
Lucinda of the light hair and dark eyes.

The VW looked the way I'd lived:
Scars of eight auto accidents
and a crumpled license plate,
half falling off;
each door a different shade of topaz.
Worn tires encircled rusted chrome rims.

The car brought me closer to you,
Lucinda of the crystalline smile.

Large tractor-trailer rigs rumbled
by the bug, waking me often
from slumber at the wheel.

Lucinda of the old Rocky Mountains
and Apache earth.
I drove and cried out your name.

You led me with those eyes
that smiled a different song.
I wanted to live in them.

You led me with desert-night talks
of old times, other loves,
and the misreading of signals.

You pulled me with the words *I love you,*
muttered while drunk on gin and vermouth
and nodding out at eastside cantinas.

Lucinda of blue-white skies,
mother of sullen daughters,
how I sought you… at street corners,
shit-kicking bars
and on that wretched highway
from Berdoo to Shaky Town.

Oh, Lucinda, of the smooth music,
quiet mountain streams
and breaking of ocean waves,
of dark dresses ruffled and torn.

Of bottles smashed over heads,
knife scars and stretch marks
you tried so hard to hide.

How I sought you.

Palmas

Palmas swayed on a rickety porch
near an old eaten-up tree
and plucked at a six-string:
The guitar man of the 'hood.

Fluid fingers moved across the neck
like a warm wind across one's brow.

Each chord filled with pain,
glory and boozed-up nights.

Every note sweating.

On Saturdays, Palmas jammed with local dudes.
They played in his honor on the nights
he didn't show up.

The guitar man—so sick, so tired,
but, man, he played so sweet.

I often wondered what gave Palmas his magic.
Blues bands wanted him.
Norteño bands wanted him.
Jazz musicians called out his name
from the bandstand.

He played Wes Montgomery
as if the dude were living inside his head.

He played crisp *corridos* and *Jarocho* blues
and seemed to make Jeff Beck
float through the living room window.

Yet he didn't venture too far beyond his rickety porch.

Sometimes he sat alone in his room,
the guitar on a corner of an unmade bed.

The last I heard, he played only
when the heroin in his body
gave him a booking.

With Stone Hands and Fire Eyes

Investors in brain damage,
anemic men in grey suits
placidly await your sacrifice
on the altar of their profits.

Brown
Mexica priests,
with stone hands
and fire eyes,
stand solid
like forged iron.

Black
Mandingo warriors,
hungry cobras
in factory furnaces
strike first.
Survivors.

Black and brown.
You pursue.
Stalk.
Throwing blows
like gun-fire
conditioned
under sweaty lights

in archaic gyms,
prepared
for the last dance.

You think Ali.
You think Duran.
You think Sugar Ray,
heeding
the longing for heroes.

Voices cut through smoky
arenas like blunt knives
clamoring for a violent poetry
written in blood.

No Work Today

The sign on the door said:
"No Work Today."

I walked in anyway.

I'd be damned if I was going to spend
$2 on bus fare, an hour on potholed roads,
and face the funny looks of suburbanites
only to find there's no work.

I'd be damned.

"Give me an application."

"Sorry buddy, no jobs."

"Well, give me an application anyway."

"Hey, save yourself the trouble…
there ain't no work today,
there was no work yesterday,
and who knows what tomorrow will bring?"

"Listen, I took two buses, walked five blocks
and killed a good part of the morning getting here.
The least I should get is an application."

"I'm telling you, it would be a waste of time.
There's no work. Read my lips:
N-O-W-O-R-K."

"No, you listen!
I demand an application. It's my right.
I didn't come all this way for not to sign something.
Give me an application, man!"

The dude looked at me with a skewed eye
and handed me a form.

I took it, triumphant!

Somebody was Breaking Windows

Somebody was breaking the windows
out of a 1970s Ford.
Somebody's anger, for who knows what,
shattered the fragile mirror of sleep,
the morning silence
and chatter of birds.
A sledgehammer in both hands then crashed
onto the side of the car,
down on the hood,
through the front grill and headlights.
This Humboldt Park street screamed
in the rage of a single young man.
Nobody got out of their homes.
Nobody did anything.
The dude kept yelling
and tearing into the car.
Nobody claimed it.
I looked out of the window as he swung again.
Next to me was a woman.
We had just awakened after a night of lovemaking.
Her six-year-old daughter was asleep
on a rug in the living room.
The woman placed her arms around me
and we both watched through the louver blinds.
Pieces of the car tumbled
onto steamed asphalt.
Man hands to create it.
Man hands to destroy it.

Something about being so mad
and taking it out on a car.
Anybody's car.
I mean, cars get killed everyday.
I understood this pain.
And every time he swung down on the metal,
I felt the blue heat swim up his veins.
I sensed the seething eye staring from his chest,
the gleam of sweat on his neck,
the anger of a thousand sneers
—the storm of bright lights
into the abyss of an eyeball.
Lonely? Out of work? Out of time?
I knew this pain. I wanted to be there,
to yell out with him,
to squeeze out the violence
that gnawed at his throat.
I wanted to be the sledgehammer,
to be the crush of steel on glass,
to be this angry young man,
a woman at my side.

Alabama

DURING BLACK EMPOWERMENT ELECTIONS
ON THE ALABAMA BLACK BELT,
I CAME FACE TO FACE WITH AMERICA.

Alabama
—seared mouths speak
smothered by timbers of cedar,
blaring out the cries of a pained land.

Alabama is rained-soaked shacks
and children born into seclusion
behind walls of betrayed promises.

Alabama is air like humid hands
grabbing throats and pushing bodies
into wet earth to harvest again.

From darkened skies come storm clouds
with deadly showers chipping away
the broken gravestones of the deceased
reminders of a former life
with slave auction blocks
next to innocent kiosks in the grass,
to the obelisk monuments
for Nathan Bedford Forest, a leading Klansman,
painted over now with "Free the Black Belt."

Nurtured by rays of sun and luminous dew drops,
Power here is sought as if it were water to thirsty lips.

Alabama is green. It is red. It is black.

Beautiful foliage green,
spilling blood red,
and life-giving earth black.

Alabama is a burial ground,
an enslaved country,
that keeps calling us back.

Juchitan

I ONCE COVERED ANTI-GOVERNMENT PROTESTS
IN THIS OAXACAN COASTAL TOWN OF MEXICO.
THE YEAR WAS 1983.
MEXICAN TROOPS HAD ALREADY LANDED.

1.

In the *zocalo*, the banter of black birds rises
as the afternoon rolls in and people gather
beneath a canopy of trees, conversing
in *Didxa*, the language of the *Za*,
the first people of this land,
appearing to share the same tongue
as the black birds.

This place is so removed from home—and so close.
Of tropical scents, brightly-woven *huipiles*
and a melodic language whispered
by children at play, women relating the news,
drunks brawling over obscure points.

The odor of beef heads—eyes bulging—
pieces of their flesh grilled in open taco stands,
satiates the humid air.
Tehuanas, wide Indian women, with hearty
laughs and round faces, prepare fish
and iguanas for the marketplace.

I slice a path through the dampness,
through the children's giggles and whimpers,
and the singing discourse of black birds.

2.
White metal benches fill with young lovers,
the elderly and sleepy-eyed.
Teenagers scamper past in T-shirts that say:
Juchitan: Capital del Mundo
—Juchitan: Capital of the World.

Every scraped eye, every hungry cry,
finds shape and hue in Juchitan.
Every oppressors fear, every liberator's spear,
is dancing and playing in Juchitan.

Harried merchants call to one another.
A young mother pokes out a brown breast.
Across the street government troops
calmly cradle machine guns.

3.
A pile of rocks lie near a large bell
on top of the "municipal palace"—city hall.
From here, the movement of troops is studied.
At signs of attack the bell is to be tolled
—to call out *'tecos* from *milpas*, huts,
and the marketplace. They have no weapons.
Save sticks. Save rocks.

Brightly dressed natives line up for hours
in front of ballot boxes—the voting is today.
Government supporters have beaten
two foreign journalists, accused of truth.
Truckloads of paid voters come in shifts.

The 'tecos march on muddy paths,
past thatch-roofed homes, in protest.
Late at night, troops move closer.
I'm stuck on the *palacio's* third floor,
next to the bell.

Journalists are told to leave.
I pick up a rock.

4.
"They're going to kill you,"
a taxi driver informs me.
It's 4 am. All night long the government
ruling party has been feasting. Armed guards
protect the revelry, a celebration dressed in lies.

The government has stolen the elections.
Earlier thousands of 'tecos assembled at the *palacio*
to hear their enraged representatives
in the music of the *Zapoteco* oratory,
extolling their centuries-old war of liberation.

"I know," I tell the taxi driver,
"but take me to the bus station anyway."
It's not safe for sympathetic *gringos*,

even if brown, to stay around.
I carry the *Juchitecos'* struggle
in a journal and in film.

The taxi driver looks at me with a question mark
on his face, then laughs.
"You must be crazier than I am," he says,
taking my bag. I clinch the camera.

A lone pig wobbles along a dirt road.

Overtown 1984

I WORKED IN MIAMI ONCE.
AT THE TIME A JURY HAD ACQUITTED
A POLICEMAN FOR KILLING AN
AFRICAN AMERICAN YOUNG MAN.
AN UPRISING FOLLOWED.

Overtown—you are the last shred of America
　　left in America.
You are the last ones to remain mute
　　in the face of destruction.
You are the long evening descended
　　into daybreak.
From the sockets of burning skulls
　　come screams of retribution.
For our sons, our daughters,
　　for fathers forced into not being fathers,
　　for mothers who only see the world
　　through the tunnel of a child's long wail.

You woke up to an inferno nightmare,
　　carrying me with you;
You with a face of flames, sweat across furrowed
　　foreheads.
You, the bones of a dark time,
　　of a stumbling down dilapidated steps.
It seemed an act of desperation, you alone
　　against the Miami skies.

Alone in the shadow of palm trees.
Alone against the blackened batons
       of police power.
Alone against the newspapers & TV stations
       & suited officials at bus stops &
       politicians in marbled corridors,
       who dared to call you "criminals."
Newspapers carried pictures of Overtown
       residents in paddy wagons, looking dejected,
pawns of a game not of their making.
But you were not alone. Your long night took me in.

I watched the burning from outside my hotel
       room following the acquittal of a police
       officer who killed an unarmed Overtown boy.
Walking toward you, helmeted officers met my quest
with shouts and orders, with whirling lights and road
blocks.
       I kept coming.
Near some apartments a boy started a fire.
The blaze was a brother of Watts, Detroit,
       The Hough and Harlem.
Near a place of murder, along a cement path,
       life came to life.
Beneath the streetlamps, under viaducts,
       below green palms, the darkness became
       glowy and red.
The voices of children rose up
       like thunderous sonatas.

Tomatoes

The poem draws from
an account that
appeared in a California
Central Valley newspaper

When you bite deep into the core
of ripe juicy tomato, sing a psalm
for Margarito Lupercio.

Praise the 17-year existence
of an immigrant tomato picker.

But don't bother to look for his fingerprints
on the thin tomato skins.

They are implanted on the banks
of the Delta Mendota Canal, embedded
on soft soil where desperate fingers
grasped and pulled, reaching out
to silent shadows on shore
as deadly jaws of rushing water
pulled him to its belly.

Margarito had jumped in so he could keep working,
to escape miserly taunts, stares of disdain,
indignities of alienhood,
to escape
Border Patrol officers tearing across
a tomato field like cowboys,

to escape
the iron bars of desert cells
and hunger's dried up face.

A brother of the fields heard Margarito's cries
as the Migra officers watched
and did nothing.

He tied together torn sheets, shirts, loose rope
—anything he could find, pleading for help
in the anxious tones that
overcome language barriers.

Officers in your name watched
and did nothing.

Workers later found Margarito's body
Wedged in the entrails of a sluice gate.
They delivered him to town,
tomato capital of the world,
awakened now, suddenly,
to the tyranny of indifference.

Piece by Piece

Piece by piece
They tear at you:
Peeling away layers of being,
Lying about who you are,
Speaking for your dreams.

In the squalor of their eyes
You are an outlaw.
Dressing you in a jacket of lies
—tailor made in steel—
You fit their perfect picture.

Take it off!
Make your own mantle.
Question the interrogators.
Eyeball the death in their gaze.
Say you won't succumb.
Say you won't believe them
When they rename you.
Say you won't accept their codes,
Their colors, their putrid morals.

Here you have a way.
Here you can sing victory.
Here you are not a conquered race
Perpetual victim
—the sullen face in a thunderstorm.

Hands/minds, they are carving out
A sanctuary. Use these weapons
Against them. Use your given gifts
—they are not stone.

Walk Late Chicago

From a night at
a Chicago homeless shelter

Walk late, this cold town,
walk late and see those who
have nothing to do but walk.
Who have to walk to stay alive,
who walk the pot-holed scarred streets
to a second's safety of alleys,
littered with rat carcasses,
to abandoned buildings
and heaps of cardboard and cloth.

Walk late in zero weather,
zero less than a number,
less than the loneliest day.
This is zero less than a heartbeat,
of no tomorrows. A deep, sickening
empty zero of late night walks
through this wind-swept constellation of lights.

On a damp corner snow is piled
black and white to the edge
of a soot-and-red brick building.
Here is the only hope still burning
this late night, of this late walk.

Come in, brother. Keep warm, brother.
What's your name, brother?
You've been here before?
You're in luck. One place here for you.
You got a name? Hey it's okay.
There's room. What's your name?

I had a name once, it meant something... once.
But now what's a name. What's a smile,
a good laugh, when all there is zero,
less than the darkest shadow
of the darkest corner
I've ever laid in.

Okay, brother, please follow me.
I walk slow, tired, stepping over mattresses,
stepping over humanity, crowded
into a converted warehouse, laden with men
—women and children in another room.

I enter a dark cavern.
On the ceiling are rows of pipes
and tracks of what used to carry
overhead cranes.
On the ground are more bodies,
a few on beds, most on the floor.
Somebody tells me to pull a mattress
from a pile. Tells me to walk over
to a corner of this dark warehouse.

Boils on flesh. Coughing deep bloody coughs.
Whispering voices. Hollering.
They say I'm mad, but this is madness.

On a crowded corner I throw the mattress
on a small empty spot near a red-faced
lice-infested man coughing up TB.
I take off my shoes, lay them next to a wall,
look up into a statue of Jesus
with outstretched hands
and imploring eyes of painted plaster.

Sleep. Bed bugs play havoc on skin.
Sleep. Sleep of tension.
Sleep like no other sweet sleep.
Sleep of zero.

Early—6 am—darkness still bathing
the warehouse. Voices break up
the glory of sleep.
Get up, everybody. Get up. Time to go.

Slowly I pick up whatever belongs to me.
Possessions? Don't laugh.
Shoes still there, wrapped in a beanie cap.
Praise to shoes!

I make my way into a loading dock area,
crowded now, standing around. I stare at faces,
talk about the latest Cub's game…
the Pope's last visit.

People in front pass out coffee
and a granola bar.
Women can be heard now,
a couple of children standing near.

Soon the dock's metal doors creak open.
Vans with daily newspapers wait outside,
ready to take those who can hawk them
on street corners and entrances
to rush-hour expressways.

While some jump into the vans,
others walk on to find a warm place
'til the day shelters open, hours still.
I feel the sting as the wet cold
slaps across my face.

Holding on to a near-empty
cup of coffee,
I enter a heartless dawn.

The Calling

FIRST WRITTEN AT 16
WHILE SITTING IN MURDERER'S ROW
OF THE HALL OF JUSTICE JAIL
IN LOS ANGELES

The calling came to me while I languished
in my room, while I whittled away my youth
in jail cells and damp *barrio* fields.

It brought me to life, out of captivity,
in a street-scarred and tattooed place
I called body.

Until then I waited silently,
a deafening clamor in my head,
but voiceless to all around,
hidden from America's eyes,
a brown boy without a name,

I would sing into a solitary
tape recorder, music never to be heard.
I would write my thoughts
in scrambled English;
I would take photos in my mind
—plan out new parks, bushy green, concrete free,
new places to play and think.

Waiting. Then it came. The calling.
It brought me out of my room.
It forced me to escape night captors
in street prisons.

It called me to war, to be writer,
to be scientist and march with the soldiers
of change.

It called me from the shadows, out of the wreckage
of my *barrio*—from among those
who did not exist.

I waited all of 16 years for this time.
Somehow, unexpected, I was called.

Acknowledgments

PRIOR TO FIRST PUBLICATION, some of the poems in this collection (sometimes in different versions) appeared in: *Scars: American Poetry in the Face of Violence*, edited by Cynthia Dubin Edelberg; *Distinct Voices: A Multicultural Anthology for English as a Second Language Writers*, edited by Jose A. Carmona; *Cool Salsa: Bilingual Poems on Growing Up Latino in the United States*, edited by Lori M. Carlson; *Espacios: Cultura y Sociedad* (Spanish & English); *Slam Poetry: Heftige Dichtung Aus Amerika* (German translation); *After Aztlan: Latino Writers in the '90s*, edited by Ray Gonzalez; *Crossroads Magazine*; *Witness Magazine*; *Americas Review*; *River Styx*; *Obras: A Publication of the Beyond Baroque Foundation*; *Contact II*; *Left Curve*; *Poetry East*; *Compages*; *Tribuno del Pueblo*; *Bulletin of El Centro de Estudios Puertorriquenos of Hunters College, New York City*; *San Fernando Poetry Journal*; *Poetry Connection*; *Dial-A-Poem Chicago*.

THANKS TO Deborah Pintonelli, Reginald Gibbons, Jack Hirschman, David Hernandez, Richard Bray, Lew Rosenbaum, Carlos Cumpian, Michael Warr, Gregorio Gomez and the "Weeds" and "Gallery Cabaret" poets. Also thanks to the members of the Los Angeles Latino Writers Association, Theater Workers Project of the United Steelworkers Local 1845, and the Latino Chicago Theater Company, who before 1989 helped bring some of these works to life. And much gratitude to Liturgy Training Publications, at the time part of the Archdiocese of Chicago, for use of time and equipment.

A SPECIAL THANKS to my wife, Maria Trinidad Rodriguez, for her patience and support.

THIS BOOK WON a 1989 Poetry Center Book Award, San Francisco State University. Thanks to all the people at the Poetry Center and judge, Jimmy Santiago Baca. And partly due to the book I was chosen in 1989 as one of the "Next Generation" of writers for the PEN International gatherings in Toronto and Montreal.

FOR THE 25TH ANNIVERSARY EDITION, I acknowledge the powerful support I've received over the years for my poetry and other endeavors from Adrienne Rich, Wanda Coleman, Raul Salinas, David Hernandez, and Jose Montoya, all of whom have recently passed. And the late Alexander Taylor who helped my future work achieve levels of success I never imagined. Rest in peace dear poets, mentors, friends.

IN 25 YEARS, Luis J. Rodriguez has been recognized as a leading Chicano poet, journalist, memoirist, children's book writer, and fiction writer—and one of the country's important thinkers, activists and innovators. He not only carved out an undeniable place in American letters with 15 books published by such distinguished presses as Touchstone/Simon & Schuster, HarperCollins, Seven Stories, Lee & Low, and Curbstone, among others—he's helped establish a community-based cultural center and bookstore, Tia Chucha's Centro Cultural, among other nonprofits addressing youth development, literature and the arts.

Also with the advent of *Poems across the Pavement,* Luis founded a small cross-cultural press that has produced the works of important U.S. poets such as Patricia Smith, Terrance Hayes, Jose Antonio Rodriguez, A. Van Jordan, Tony Fitzpatrick, Kyoko Mori, Virgil Suarez, Luivette Resto, and Elizabeth Alexander.

Today Tia Chucha Press is distributed by the prestigious Northwestern University Press and has published more than 50 poetry collections, anthologies, chapbooks, and a CD. Formerly based in Chicago, the press is now a project of Tia Chucha's Centro Cultural in the San Fernando Valley section of Los Angeles.

Tia Chucha Press in 2012 published its first non poetry book, *Rushing Waters, Rising Dreams: How the Arts are Transforming a Community,* edited by Luis J. Rodriguez and Denise Sandoval, documenting the powerful changes through the arts in the poor and working class Northeast San Fernando Valley. John F. Cantu wrote and directed a documentary film of the same name, produced by Tia Chucha's Centro Cultural.

Chief among Luis's contributions is the best-selling memoir of gang life, *Always Running, La Vida Loca, Gang Days in L.A.,* which has sold close to half a million copies and won the Carl Sandburg Book Award, a New York Times' Notable Book, and the Chicago Sun-Times Book Award. Not only is *Always Running* one of the most checked out books in libraries, it is one of the most stolen. His latest book is the sequel, *It Calls You Back: An Odyssey Through Love, Addiction, Revolutions and Healing,* a finalist for a National Book Critics Circle Award.